Car Accident Injury
PERSONAL INJURY & ACCIDENT LAWYER

CAR ACCIDENT INJURY: ATTORNEY OR LAWYER NECESSARY?

Law Offices of Lisa Douglas
2300 Main
North Little Rock, AR 72114
501-798-0004
739 South 7th Street
Suite 2
Heber Springs, AR 72543
www.LisaGDouglas.com

DISCLAIMER

This Book is Not Legal Advice

This information is general in nature and should not be relied on as a substitute for legal advice.

This book is provided as an education service by Law Offices of Lisa Douglas.

 Law Offices of Lisa Douglas, PLLC ———

TABLE OF CONTENTS

Foreward iv

Why This Book? 1

Insurance Companies: Tricks of The
    Trade 3

What is a Personal Injury Case? 5

Proof: Whose Fault Is It? 5

Do You Need An Attorney To Settle Your
    Case? 6

Guilt Factor 8

What is My Case Worth? 9

Giving a Recorded Statement to the
    Insurance Company 10

Protecting My Right To Compensation 10

Mistakes Made When Dealing With Your
    Doctors After the Injury 13

Four Deadly Sins That Can Wreck Your Case .. 17

A Note From the Author 19

I Do Not Accept the Following Cases 21

FOREWORD

**If you can answer YES to the following questions,
I may be the lawyer for you.**

1.   Do you have anticipated medical bills and lost wages of approximately $2,000?

2.   Is there visible damage to your vehicle?

3.   Was the accident the other driver's fault?

4.   Did you receive medical treatment immediately or shortly after the accident?

5.   Have you received the treatment your medical doctor prescribed and followed your medical doctor's recommendations?

6.   Did the accident occur less than three years ago?

**If you can answer YES to each of these questions,
give Lisa Douglas a call at
501-798-0004**

WHY THIS BOOK?

I wrote this book because, if you are like most, this is the first time you have been involved in an accident and you have many questions. Many times I have found the questions come too late and, as a result, the injured victim pays because his or her lack of information.

By now, you are receiving calls from the insurance company adjuster eager to ask you some questions and obtain a taped statement from you about the accident. The first thing that you should never forget is that the insurance company has virtually unlimited resources to carry out it's main mission: to avoid paying you or pay you as little as possible.

The insurance company may be asking you to sign a few forms so they can get your records and "handle everything for you." The insurance company may have already proposed you settle your claim by offering you money. These types of offers are tempting, but BEWARE. Before you accept the money, the insurance company will require you to sign a release form. This form forever releases the insurance company and the driver who caused the wreck from any further obligation to you.

You started your search for an attorney, but you did not find the advertising helped you decide which attorney was best for you. As you continued your search, you realized all of the ads say virtually the same thing.

I wrote this book for **you.** Hopefully you will find it will give you some valuable information to consider on your own time BEFORE you hire an attorney and before you talk to the insurance company's adjuster.

This book is too limited to explore every issue or address each possible question you may have.

Further, this book is not intended to give legal advice and nothing in this book is legal advice. Obtaining this book from me does not create an attorney-client relationship between us. I do not sign up everyone who calls my office that has been involved in an accident.

Insurance Companies: Tricks of the Trade

The insurance adjuster works for the insurance company — not for you. Their job is to keep money for the insurance company.

Tactics used by Insurance companies:

1. Delay.

2. Confusing those who have claims.

3. Disputing medical treatment.

4. Acting like your friend and making false promises.

The adjuster's goal is to settle for as little money as possible. Therefore, you should be very cautious in relying on the adjuster to estimate the value of your claim.

Resist the pressure to settle immediately. Insurance companies may attempt to settle in the first few telephone conversations to get you to settle for a small amount. You should resist this temptation to settle before you are fully aware of the extent of the injuries you have.

Some adjusters may attempt to settle your bodily injury claim before you have been released from treatment. There are some companies that will contact you within 24 hours of reporting the accident, attempting to get you to settle your claim for a small amount. It is usually best to find out the extent and nature of your injuries and complete treatment, before you consider settlement.

Remember that you and the insurance company are on opposite sides. Both sides have different goals. You want what is best for you and they want what is best for them. When you understand how things work, it is much easier to achieve what is best for you. What you don't know about the personal injury claims process can hurt you.

What is a Personal Injury Claim?

A personal injury claim is a claim where you were physically injured due to someone else's carelessness. If only your car was banged up, you do not have personal injury claim. That is, a property damage claim. But if both you and your car were injured, then you have a personal injury claim and a property damage claim.

So, there are two parts to a claim: (1) personal injury, *i.e.* physical injuries to your body; (2) property damage; *i.e.* damage to your automobile or other property. These claims are generally addressed separately with the insurance company.

PROOF: Whose Fault Is It?

Just because you were injured in a motor vehicle accident does not mean you are entitled to recover anything. The question of who caused the accident forms the basis of the determination of who is the responsible party. The answer to this question usually determines who has to pay for all or part of injuries.

A police report can often provide overwhelming evidence of carelessness by documenting that the driver disobeyed a specific law and this violation caused the accident.

Do You Need An Attorney To Settle
Your Accident Case?

You do not need an attorney to settle every small claim. Usually small claims involve little to no damage to the vehicle and the treatment for the injury lasts as little as a few weeks. In these types of cases, the medical bills are usually less than two thousand dollars and the injuries will not be permanent.

In smaller cases, it may be more cost effective for you to settle your own case; otherwise, part of what your attorney recovers will be used to pay an attorney's fee.

However, in consenting to a settlement offer from the insurance company you are assuming that the degree of your injuries has been fully determined. When you accept a settlement offer from the insurance company, you will be required to sign a release. This release is legally designed to permanently prevent any future payment, even if your medical condition deteriorates or the injuries were worse than you previously thought. Therefore, you should be absolutely certain you will not require future medical care before settling.

Remember, insurance companies are usually large, multi-million dollar corporations whose goal is to make a profit. That means they maximize profits by minimizing pay outs to the injured victim.

Studies show that an insurance company will invariably try and pay you less than your injury deserves.

Opposing insurance adjusters will frequently ask if you have a lawyer yet. If you are not represented by an attorney, the adjuster will probably say: "That is good news. Because retaining a lawyer does not increase the value of your case. In fact, a lawyer will take one-third of your settlement, plus costs. I am so relieved a lawyer is not involved and you and I can work this out together."

Research conducted by the insurance industry shows that the insurance industry saves money when the injured victim is not represented by a lawyer. The less informed you are, the better they like it.

In reality, the insurance companies hate it when you retain a lawyer to protect your rights, because the adjusters at the insurance company know they will have to deal with someone who has knowledge of the personal injury system. They know the lawyer will not let the insurance company take advantage of the client. Consulting a lawyer early in the process can help you avoid many of the pitfalls.

Guilt Factor

In order to obtain compensation for your damages, the insurance industry offers you money. They do not make the other driver apologize to you, they do not take away his/her license, and they do not send him/her to a school to learn how to drive more safely.

Because the compensation comes down to money, the insurance companies have devised ways to avoid paying you. The level of their success in evading payments on claims can be judged by looking at their assets and profits.

The United States insurance industry receives over $1 trillion dollars every year in premiums. It has approximately $3.8 trillion dollars in assets. In fact, for the past decade, the insurance industry has annually averaged over $30 billion in profits. (www.iii.org)

What is My Case Worth?

The value of any injury case is determined by the severity of the injury/injuries and damages suffered by the injured party. Damages include medical expenses, lost wages, loss of the ability to work, property damage, pain, suffering, mental anguish, and disfigurement.

Giving a Recorded Statement to
the Insurance Company

One tactic of the insurance industry is to contact the injured victim immediately after the accident to obtain a recorded statement. This is one of the first ways you can hurt your case. This recorded statement can be used against you to minimize or even deny your claim. In fact it can be detrimental to your claim to give a recorded statement without full understanding of what is really going on.

Protecting My Right To Compensation

The following is a list of the problems I frequently encounter where the injured victim failed to do one or all of these and this failure adversely impacted the case. This list is not an exhaustive list and is not intended to be. There is not enough time to cover every conceivable problem.

1. *Write Everything Down.* Don't just depend on your memory. Write everything down about the accident as soon as possible. Having these notes to rely on seven to ten months after the fact will prove far more helpful than relying solely on your memory. Take photographs.

2. *Notes about your Injuries.* In the days following your accident, keep a diary of pains, aches, cramps, cricks, distress, irritation, misery, soreness, spasm, strain, tenderness or discomforts your injuries cause. Also writing these down will help you remember to report them to your medical provider at your next appointment. If there are visible cuts, marks, scratches, or bruises, take photos of these for documentation. Photos are difficult to challenge. And, as the old saying goes, "a picture is worth a thousand words."

3. *Get medical treatment immediately.* Get immediate medical treatment and let your health care provider know of all of your injuries including pain and discomfort. Right now, You are probably thinking that anyone who has been injured in an automobile accident would seek medical care, right? WRONG. Many who are injured refuse emergency medical care from the emergency medical technician at the scene of the accident or refuse to go to the emergency room to be seen by a doctor. Under these circumstances, it is much easier for the insurance adjuster to deny or even diminish the value of your claim. Your explanation that you did not know how badly you were injured will be difficult to sell.

You have to be able to show that your injuries were caused by the crash. Medical records documenting your injuries are the proof you need. By receiving an examination by the doctor immediately after the accident you obtain the documentation you need to assist you in your claims process.

Failing to seek medical attention can and likely will, weaken your case.

4. *Communicate the pain and discomfort you are experiencing from your injuries.* The best way to communicate your injuries to the insurance company is through documentation in your medical records. When you visit your health care provider make sure to tell them of all of your aches, pain, stiffness, and discomforts you are experiencing as a result of your injury. Your medical records are very important in determining how badly you have been injured; therefore, if it is not contained within your medical records, it didn't happen. So, make sure you tell the health care provider about your injuries.

Mistakes Made When Dealing With
Your Doctor After the Injury

✓ *Failing to receive immediate, or bare minimum next day, medical attention after the motor vehicle accident.* You are responsible for proving that you were injured as a result of the accident. It is a commonly held belief that if you aren't hurt badly enough to seek immediate medical attention, then you weren't hurt that bad and the settlement offer will reflect that belief. The longer you delay treatment, the less believable your complaints of injury will be viewed. "Because after all if you were really injured, you would have seen a doctor right away." Whiplash, for example, does not always show up immediately, but it should within days. The bottom line is you should see the doctor as soon as possible. You don't want the adjuster or the insurance attorney arguing that you couldn't have been hurt too badly, because after all you didn't even bother to see a doctor for two weeks.

✓ *Missing or Showing Up Late For Medical Appointments.* Your medical records for the treatment you received as a result of the accident will be reviewed by the insurance adjuster. When you miss an appointment your medical record normally just says "did not show." Failing to make two or more appointments could be construed as you are not committed to getting better. You don't want the adjuster or the insurance attorney saying, you can't be hurting that much because after all, you didn't even make all of your appointments.

✓ *Failing to Have Your Pain Accurately Documented in Your Medical Records.* Insurance Companies and possible potential jurors are not inclined to believe you are experiencing pain just because you say so. They want to see documentation of it in your medical records. Because after all, if you were in so much pain, you would have informed your doctor and he or she would have documented it in your medical records. One way to help make sure your complaints of pain, discomfort or limitations make it into your medical records is for you to write it out before you visit your doctor or health care provider. That way you don't have to depend only on your memory to recall the details. You could even give this list to your doctor in an attempt to insure they document your complaints in your medical record.

✓ *Failing to Tell Your Doctor if Your Injury is Affecting Your Ability to Work.* Insurance Companies and possible potential jurors are not inclined to believe that your injury prevented you from working just because you say so. If the injury is affecting your job performance, it is important for you to tell this to your doctor. This way you obtain documentation and the doctor could give you time off work or restrict your activity at work. The insurance company will look for this to validate any time off from work. If you took time off without a doctor's excuse then this time off will not be considered valid because it was not authorized by your doctor, therefore it does not count. Because after all, if you needed time off, the doctor would have written you an excuse for the time off from work. Otherwise, this time off was merely self imposed and does not count.

✓ *Failing to Take Medications as Prescribed.* If the doctor prescribed medication for you, there is a reason. You should follow your doctor's instructions. If you are unable to tolerate the medication, tell your doctor immediately. Perhaps he or she can prescribe something else that is more agreeable with you or the doctor can discontinue the current prescription.

Choosing not to follow the doctor's instructions can destroy your claim.

✓ *Stopping Medical Treatment Too Soon.* It is a commonly held belief that if a person stops receiving medical treatment for his/her injury, then they are no longer injured, but now they are healed. If there are significant gaps in treatment, this suggests you are healed from the initial injury and must have received a new injury that was caused by something other than the motor vehicle accident. The doctor should be the one who releases you from further treatment or tells you there is nothing more that can be done to improve your condition.

✓ *Failing to Follow Prescribed Treatment for Depression or Anxiety.* It is not uncommon for an accident victim to experience depression and anxiety following an accident. Sometimes treatment is needed. Normally, insurance companies usually only compensate if these conditions are properly diagnosed and treated by medical professionals.

✓ *Failing to Keep a File.* It is important to keep track of every medical care provider that treated you after a motor vehicle accident. Keeping track of these documents as well as any other paperwork or bills that pertains to the accident will help reduce the work at the end of the claim.

Four Deadly Sins That Can Wreck Your Case

1. *The Lawyer Refers the Client to a Specific Doctor or Specific Chiropractor.*

This could be the kiss of death to a claim. This type of referral relationship not only creates suspicion, but the necessity of the treatment could be viewed as suspicious too. How believable do you think a doctor's testimony would be if the jury finds out this doctor also treated 30 other clients referred to him/her by this same lawyer in the past year?

2. *Hiding Previous Motor Vehicle Accidents From Your Lawyer.*

The other side will be interested in knowing how many other motor vehicle accidents you have been involved in. In fact they probably already know.

If you have been involved in prior motor vehicle accidents, your attorney can determine if this creates a problem in your current claim.

3.   *Hiding Other Injuries*

You must be open and up front with your attorney regarding other injuries. If you received treatment for this other injury, there will be a record of this. The insurance company could find this record. Your lawyer can deal with this if they are made aware of it.

4.   *Misrepresenting Your Activity Level*

Insurance companies hire private investigators to investigate areas just like this. If you say that your activity level is substantially diminished as a result of the injury and then are taped hiking a mountain, you can forget about your claim.

A Note From the Author

After reading this book, I hope you have more insight about the personal injury claims process than when you initially requested this book and began your investigation. This book will give you a head start and get you thinking about the things that can affect your claim. My purpose in writing this book was to equip you with general information about how personal injury cases work and provide you with some things you should know to increase the chances of winning yours. After all, knowledge is power.

Please understand that I do not accept every case about which I am contacted. I carefully select the few cases that I will accept at any one time. This way I am better able to focus on maximizing my client's recoveries.

I Do Not Accept The Following Cases

In an attempt to provide personal service and focus on maximizing my client's recoveries I decline cases which do not meet certain criteria. Therefore, as a general rule, I do not accept the following types of cases:

❏ Cases with pre-existing injury that is the same as or similar to the injury complained of in this accident. For example; if your medical history included three prior back surgeries, the chances of recovering a substantial amount of compensation for the same back injury will be very low. I do not feel it is worth the risk to the client to pursue these types of cases.

❏ Cases where the statute of limitations is less than three months away.

❏ I do not take accident cases where the potential client has been ticketed for violating the motor vehicle law.